Soul Fire
Awakening to the Power of Divine Love

Bill Frase

ISBN: 979-8-6716-3548-5

CONTENTS

ACKNOWLEDGMENTS

There are no words for my gratitude to my Heavenly Parent for blessing me with Unconditional Love. I am in awe of Your Wisdom and Generosity.

I want to express my heartfelt gratitude to my partner, Wendy, for being a faithful sounding board and her love, support, feedback, and abundant patience. I wouldn't be here without you.

I am deeply thankful for the inspiration, love, and blessings of the angels of Divine Love who have helped bring this work into being despite my ignorance, resistance, challenges, and limitations.

I am deeply grateful for all who provided feedback and support at different stages in this book's development. My thanks go to Eva Peck, Elizabeth Morana, Jane Gartshore, Penny Morse, Terry Adler, Catherine Kent, and Al Fike for their ideas and feedback.

I especially want to thank Beth Mazur for her feedback and efforts to share the truth of soul-awakening through the power of Divine Love. I hope this book will play a part in that effort.

I believe that everyone's love and feedback have made this book more helpful than it would have been otherwise. All errors of commission and omission are mine alone.

1. WELCOME

I have written this book to help you awaken to the power of the Creator's Soul Fire of Divine Love by learning how to receive it. The words, Soul Fire, encapsulate my practice and experience of seeking and receiving the power of Divine Love. Soul Fire also represents the burning desire of our Creator for union with us. Soul Fire ignites our passions, perceptions, and potentials. Soul Fire blazes trails through our tangled and dismal inner swamps, leading us into joyful union with our Heavenly Parent.

This book distills the essential steps and insights needed to support your soul's desire for spiritual awakening. If you do as I suggest, you will experience the renewal of your soul regardless of religion, race, ethnicity, impairments, sexual orientation, age, gender identity, addictions, sex, mistakes, political affiliations, habits, triggers, egotism, shame, excuses, intelligence, socio-economic status, caste, social roles, or any other category, quality, or circumstance that anyone could ever use as an excuse not to seek soul transformation.

There is nothing that can prevent anyone who desires the Soul Fire of Divine Love from being remade by it. Please read that sentence again and let it sink into the core of your being. It is the truth around which everything in this book revolves. If you consistently act on this truth, your life will be forever changed.

If you do as I suggest, you will be transformed by the Soul Fire that burns within the Creator's Heart.

The steps of the soul-awakening process are simple and few. They have not been easy for me. I hope that taking these steps will be easier for you. Soul-awakening is not a fancy or glamorous process. If you have not been seeking the Soul Fire of Divine Love, much of this information may be new.

I hope you will do the work of waking up your soul long enough to be convinced that Divine Love is real and powerful. I'm begging you to do everything you can to begin the process and stick with it no matter what! If you ever become discouraged in your quest for spiritual transformation, please contact me, and I will do my best to help! If you engage in this process with patient persistence, you will be rewarded in ways beyond your wildest imaginings and your highest hopes.

2. MY STORY

I was the first of four children born to an earnest and hardworking couple in the American Midwest. I was a sensitive child who loved nature and *Star Wars*. I wanted to be smart and please the people in my life. I felt like I achieved mixed results on both of those fronts.

I often felt that there was something wrong with the world. I had many experiences where I said to myself, *This is not how it's supposed to be! There has to be a better way! One way or another, I'm going to figure it out!*

In my early twenties, I unexpectedly entered into an altered state of awareness, unlike anything I had experienced before. This mystical experience showed me that there were realities beyond the limits of my knowledge, concepts, and imagination.

This defining moment of my life catapulted me on a quest to understand what had happened and what it meant. After years of seeking the truth without much success, I became mired in self-loathing. I had done my best to distract myself from these unpleasant thoughts and emotions, but my old tactics weren't working anymore. As my self-hatred intensified, I started experiencing disturbing sensations of tightness in my chest.

I was afraid that I would be saddled with this pain and suffering for the rest of my existence. I saw no way out. Eventually, deep within me, I had the tiniest hope that there was an answer to my problem. After feeling this glimmer of hope, I found and applied information that put me on the path of soul-awakening through the power of Divine Love. After a few months, the pain that caused me so much concern was gone, never to return.

By doing the practice described in this book, my life has transformed. I now have a sense of wholeness, peace, and purpose that was missing for much of my life. Instead of suffering in resistance and regret, I now live in joy and gratitude for the blessings I receive every day.

I'm not special or unique, except in the way that everyone is special and unique. Anyone may do what I have done and much more. Every day, I ask for my Creator's Soul Fire and the blessings that come with it. My requests are always granted. I'm sure that your heartfelt requests will be rewarded as well.

3. ORIENTATION

We are entering subtle realities that are not well known or understood. I offer the following descriptions as an orientation to this unseen world.

Creator - Heavenly Parent - Source

The Creator is the Ultimate Spiritual Reality that brings everything and everyone into being. The Source is all-powerful, all-knowing, and all-loving. Our Heavenly Parent radiates the Essence of Divine Love throughout the cosmos because of a great desire for union with every soul.

Soul

The soul is our spiritual core or essence. It's our true self. The soul is the Creator's child. Unlike our Heavenly Parent, our soul is a finite creation and not divine. Our soul chooses, free from external compulsion. Our soul desires to receive love and to express love freely according to our unique makeup. There are two ways to do this. We may remove the impediments to love or replace our original nature with the Uncreated Nature of the Source. Through receiving the essence of Divine Love, we may experience a conscious union with our Heavenly Parent while retaining a radically altered sense of individuality.

Divine Love - Soul Fire - Ultimate Power - Uncreated Essence - The Gift

The Heavenly Parent's nature is Divine Love. It's an uncreated power that may be received by anyone who desires it, gradually changing the soul from a natural creature into a divine being. When received in abundance, it is the only substance capable of giving us conscious knowledge of our spiritual immortality and oneness with the Creator.

Soul-Awakening - Spiritual Transformation - Soul Transformation

Spiritual transformation, soul transformation, and soul-awakening are interchangeable terms for the same process. These phrases refer to an ongoing, eternal journey. Engaging in this endeavor requires our desire and choice to receive Divine Love. This undertaking fundamentally changes us by gradually replacing the soul's created nature with the Source's Uncreated Essence.

Material Mind - Mind - Intellect - Artificial Intelligence - Inner-AI - AI

The material mind includes all of our mental and emotional functions that are not essential to the soul's functioning. The mind's original purpose was to support the soul's purpose after its incarnation. Today our intellect is like an overdeveloped Artificial Intelligence application that overshadows and suppresses our soul's perceptions and expressions. It desires to protect and advance us by resisting life and refusing to love. We often identify with the mind's troubling attitudes and images. Our fear-based thoughts, emotions, and forms are the building blocks of the fabricated world.

Fabricated World - Pseudo-Reality

The fabricated world includes all aspects of existence that humanity has created and perpetuated through our refusal to love and our resistance to life. These fabrications manifest as numerous and persistent facts that are not in harmony with love, truth, beauty, and goodness. This illusion consists of humanity's distorted perceptions and dysfunctional results. The fabricated world is an immersive, temporary pseudo-reality built upon and sustained by humankind's gross resistance. It's an unpleasant, auto-generated, interactive simulation of perceptions, emotions, and manifestations. Most of us experience the fabricated world as reality, even though it has no existence independent of humanity.

Material

When we think of material things, we tend to think of forms of energy that have coalesced into observable forms of matter. While this is true, materiality also includes everything that is not spiritual.

Spiritual

Everything that is not material is spiritual. The soul and its energies that express its agency and desires are spiritual. All that belongs to the Creator's Being and the highest spiritual realms beyond the many layers of the material universe are spiritual.

Natural

Everything created by the Heavenly Parent that is not part of the Creator's being is a part of nature.

Divine

The Creator is divine, as well as those who choose to receive the Creator's Uncreated Essence.

4. THE WAY OF SOUL-AWAKENING

Here are the steps of the spiritual transformation process reduced to their most basic form. If you are ever challenged by any of the details and distinctions in this book, please refer back to these three simple steps and do them.

1. **Ask for Divine Love.**
2. **Always, Always, Always Love.**
3. **Again!**

The way of soul-awakening is simple. If you engage in these steps regardless of what you believe, think, hope, or know, you will experience the power of Divine Love.

It may take seconds to years before you know that something beautiful is happening to you. However long it takes for you to perceive feedback on your unique path of soul-awakening is more than worth it. Any amount of time and effort invested in transforming your soul produces an infinite return of benefits throughout eternity. Persisting with this process is an investment in your unique and priceless self.

This method is not a quick fix. It has taken each of us great effort and many years to get where we are today. It will take time and effort to experience the awakening of our souls through the power of Divine Love. Given our challenges and burdens, let's be patient with ourselves, others, and the process.

In the pages that follow, I will do my best to give you what you need to take your unique spiritual journey. If you engage persistently with the soul-awakening process, whatever you need along the way will be provided. Doing this practice attracts spiritual forces who desire to inspire, heal, empower, and protect you. If you feel alone, you are not. If you feel like you have been left behind or abandoned by life, you can still access everything you need to embark upon this transformative spiritual adventure. Help will be given when you ask from your heart. If you get off track, give up, or become lost, this process will still be available to you when you are ready, in this life or the next.

I humbly urge you to seek your spiritual transformation in Divine Love sooner rather than later. The world is undergoing massive and rapid changes. If you want to wake up, you will receive everything you need regardless of what may be happening. The world needs strong souls now more than ever. Nothing strengthens us as Divine Love does.

You have a profound opportunity to experience unexpected wonders and delights upon your path. This has been my experience. I didn't always get what I *wanted* along the way, but I received what I *needed*. What I needed has always been so much better than what I thought I wanted. May this be your experience as well. Let's jump into the steps!

5. STEP 1 - ASK FOR DIVINE LOVE

Asking for Divine Love is the first step because it's how you receive the power to awaken your soul.

In this step, asking means expressing our heartfelt desire. Asking is not just an empty exercise where we say from our mind, "Would you please give me Divine Love?" Asking for the Creator's Soul Fire flows from authentically expressing our vulnerability and openness.

We receive Divine Love when we desire it with an open heart. The expression of our soul's real desire for an intimate relationship with the Creator is an act of profound vulnerability. We allow ourselves to be vulnerable when we open our hearts and express love toward others. We are especially vulnerable when we express our desire to receive love from another. This includes expressing our willingness to receive Soul Fire from our Heavenly Parent. Unlike the risks associated with being vulnerable toward people who may betray our trust and break our hearts, opening our hearts to our Creator will never lead to injury, heartbreak, or betrayal. Our Heavenly Parent is trustworthy and will never hurt us.

There are many ways to authentically express our desire for Divine Love. The typical possibilities for consciously desiring the Creator's Essence can be grouped into two basic approaches - the Way of Poverty and the Way of Abundance. Both methods may be helpful as long as they support the authentic expression of our soul's desire for union with the Creator.

The Way of Poverty

One way of experiencing our vulnerability and openness flows from the awareness of our need, pain, stress, regrets, ignorance, or challenges. Through increased sensitivity to our perceptions of lack, we may express our sorrow, shame, fear, doubt, helplessness, and woundedness. This list only scratches the surface of the possibilities for our heartfelt expressions of deep need.

As we allow these feelings to rise to the surface, our souls may express the deep desire for closeness with our Creator beneath these raw and authentic emotions. Expressing our sincere desire for healing and wholeness invites Divine Love to pour into our soul in abundance.

The Way of Abundance

Another approach to express vulnerability and openness flows from sincere gratitude for our blessings. In this approach, we express our longing for more Divine Love and the gifts that come with it. We desire more of what we have received. In the Way of Abundance, we know that the Soul Fire supply is limitless. Our sincere yearning brings more of this Great Gift.

Expressing the Desire of Your Soul

Most souls start their path toward soul-awakening through the Way of Poverty. I started my journey of soul-awakening through the realization of my need for help. As I have continued on my path, I have become more familiar with the Way of Abundance. My gratitude for the blessings I have received helps me to open up to receive even more Divine Love. I have shared both paths to help you wherever you may be on your journey.

If we are not feeling the need to seek Divine Love from our feelings of poverty, we may desire more through our perceptions of abundance. If we are not inclined to long for Soul Fire from our sense of abundance, we may crave it through our perceptions of poverty. It is even possible to express our desire by recognizing our great need and gratitude at the same time.

The way we ask for Divine Love is not as important as doing our best to desire it from the depths of our souls with as much openness and vulnerability as possible. Please don't overthink the distinctions between the different ways to ask for Divine Love. They are not inclusive of the ways that we may express our desire for union with the Creator. There are as many different ways of opening and allowing our souls to receive the Divine Essence as there are souls.

Your soul is a unique, multidimensional entity that does not need to be limited by your mind, anyone else's thinking, or the fabricated world. Nothing can come between our Heavenly Parent and us, except what we allow. Express your heartfelt longings with authenticity, and you will receive Divine Love.

Why Must We Ask?

Why hasn't the Creator just given Divine Love to everyone in the first place? Soul Fire is an incredibly powerful gift that transforms our lives. It must be chosen to be received. If the Gift were forced upon us without our consent, it would not be a gift.

Every human being is created with a natural love that forms the essence of the soul. The soul is designed to experience and express its oneness with the natural love that pervades all creation.

Divine Love is an uncreated power that forms the Essence of the Heavenly Parent's Being. It's qualitatively different from the natural love that souls experience as part of their creation. Unlike natural love, the Divine Essence cannot be degraded or corrupted in any way. ***Divine Love is a gift of radical power. The decision to receive it represents a freely expressed desire to become one with the Creator instead of being limited to oneness with creation.*** By choosing Divine Love, you are saying, *"Creator, I don't want to be bound by the limits of my created nature any longer. I desire the unlimited possibilities of union with You."*

When we receive the Creator's Essence, we are on our way toward conscious union with our Creator. This path leads to experiences of spiritual realities far beyond the highest level of oneness with the creation that a purified soul may experience. Receiving the Creator's Substance changes the course of our lives for the better, forever. As we seek Soul Fire, our soul is transfigured from a natural creation into a divine individual that is one with the Creator's Essence of Divinity.

The Practice of Asking for Divine Love

We are individuals and will ask for Divine Love in our own way. Each soul's awakening will be unique. To discover what works best for you, play and experiment with the following possibilities as you practice "Step 1 - Ask for Divine Love."

If you are having challenges expressing your soul's desire for union or connection with the Creator, it may be helpful to long for this relationship from your heart center. It's a link to your soul.

Consider the development of a regular schedule, list of cues, rhythm, habit, or system that supports your efforts to ask for Divine Love. Seeking Soul Fire is like the in-breath for our soul. Just as we need to breathe air to live, the same goes for the souls' awakening.

It may be helpful to breathe Divine Love into your soul when you inhale *and* exhale. Breathing deeply is good for your body too!

Seek Divine Love in different places, at different times, with different people, and under different circumstances. There is nothing outside of ourselves that can prevent us from asking for and receiving the Gift. The only barriers to experiencing Soul Fire are those we choose.

Invite Divine Love into your soul with and without using words. The soul's desire is beyond the boundaries of human language, but that doesn't mean that words or thoughts may not help us express our desire for union with the Creator.

Desire Divine Love indoors and outside. Ask for it in sound and silence. Seek Soul Fire while doing other activities. Long for it while moving or in stillness. Feel free to ask with your eyes open or closed. Allow Divine Love to come with or without thought.

You may experience different perceptions and sensations while asking for Divine Love, or you may not. Whatever the case may be, it's essential to focus upon your desire for union with the Creator. Becoming distracted by or obsessed with perceptions and sensations or the lack of them does not support the soul-awakening process.

If you become aware of what other people experience when seeking Divine Love, it is helpful to refrain from making comparisons or judgments. All are unique. There is no standardized process or timetable for soul-awakening and the sensations and perceptions that may be experienced. Release yourself from the prison of your hopes and expectations. Enjoy every nuance of your one-of-a-kind adventure of soul-awakening!

Be present here and now. Soul Fire is only experienced in the present. We cannot receive it when we are focused upon the past or the future. Be here now.

Asking for Divine Love is powerful and effective as a solo activity. It is also gratifying to seek it with others in the same place or at the same time. There are groups around the world who express their desire for the Creator's Essence together regularly and experience many benefits from doing so.

Some people may be concerned that placing so much emphasis on asking for Divine Love is selfish. Love is unlimited. Receive all you can!

We can't ask for Divine Love all the time. We have other commitments and responsibilities. What we do when we're not seeking Soul Fire is the next step in our soul-awakening journey.

6. STEP 2 - ALWAYS, ALWAYS, ALWAYS LOVE

The second step of the soul-awakening process addresses what to do when we're not seeking Divine Love. Although this step is self-explanatory in its simplicity, it's not what we typically do. Is it even possible to always love? If so, why don't we? Let's explore our purpose.

We Are Made to Love

Our Creator always loves and wants us to know that we are loved. We know this when we receive Divine Love.

We have also been created in the invisible likeness of our Creator to express love. This second step reflects this fact, but we refuse to give love frequently. These decisions are behind every problem we experience.

Whenever we betray our desire to love, we do not live in harmony with our purpose and the universal principles of energy flow. Every decision to withhold love restricts the flow of love within our soul.

Think of physical health as the harmonious flow of energies throughout the body. Disease and dysfunction manifest whenever energy flow is persistently inhibited. Like the well-being that we experience as energy moves freely throughout the body, the healthy soul receives and gives love freely. When we choose not to love, we hurt our soul. Just as physical pain motivates us to seek treatment for our bodies, we may see all suffering as an opportunity for love.

If we persist in stopping the flow of love, we will continue to suffer and harm others. If we think of love as being like air for the soul, not allowing it to come into our souls is the spiritual equivalent of suffocation. Withholding love equates to holding our breath. Just as these conditions can weaken or kill us if they persist, our choices to limit the flow of love weaken our soul. Thankfully, we cannot destroy our souls no matter what we do. Our refusal to love is like placing a sleeper hold on our souls, knocking us out until we awaken to our sincere desire to receive and express love.

Let's consider how our material mind and the fabricated world provoke us to refuse love.

The Material Mind and the Fabricated World

Our material mind is supposed to follow the soul's instructions. Instead, it has become unplugged from our soul, acting like artificial intelligence (AI)[1] run amok. Unplugged from the love and wisdom of the soul,

---

[1] AI, inner-AI, artificial intelligence, mind, material mind, and intellect are all used interchangeably.

the mind only moves in two directions: toward rewards and away from threats.[2] Our inner-AI bosses us around instead of taking its cues from the soul. Whenever we react out of fear, our inner-AI has taken over, and we fail to love.

The fabricated world is the false reality manufactured by the fear-based programs of humankind. It's the battleground where the inner-AIs of humans form unsteady alliances and wage war. The fabricated world is the net result of humanity's immersive and interactive illusions. It's a false reality that screams, "It's not safe to love! Don't even try." Most of the time, we believe it.

Let's see how we refuse to love and become trapped within the lies we tell ourselves.

How We Refuse to Love

Every moment of our lives is an opportunity to give love. Occasions for love can take an infinite number of forms. Perhaps you desire to create something beautiful or useful. Do you long to serve in some way? Maybe you are curious about a new subject or relationship. You may feel compelled to gather your courage to do what is right. Breaking a bad habit could be your task. All of these and any other desires that require the rejection of short-term self-gratification to

---

[2] *Your Brain at Work*, p 105.

achieve meaningful outcomes are opportunities to love.[3]

Sometimes when we feel the desire to love, we refuse to act on it. What follows is a description of how we do this.[4]

Think of a time when you had a desire to love that you denied. This desire came from your soul. Your material mind connected this open and vulnerable expression of love with threats that needed to be avoided. Your AI correlated openness and vulnerability with pain. It wanted to protect you from yourself. How many times had you loved, only to be hurt? What about all the times you were crushed after caring too much? If you weren't careful, you could have been wounded again. This threat assessment generated by your AI was enough to cause you to betray your desire to love.

Because you know deep within your soul that your purpose is to love, you must rationalize your decision not to love. You need to tell yourself a convincing story about why you are right not to act upon your impulse to love.

What follows is a more detailed description of how we betray our desire to love. Most of this process happens instantaneously and automatically. What

---

[3] *The War of Art* - Resistance's Greatest Hits, pp 5-6.

[4] More information on self-betrayal may be found in *Leadership and Self-Deception*, *The Anatomy of Peace,* and other publications by the Arbinger Institute. Much of the information in this chapter is based upon the Arbinger Institute's publications listed under Sources.

follows is a super-slowed down depiction of how we deny our desire to love and justify our decision after the fact. Let's pretend you perceive an opportunity to love right now.

1. Your soul simply desires to love or help.
2. Your material mind senses the openness and vulnerability of your soul's desire to love and tries to predict how it can lead to pain. Over time, your AI has associated danger with your willingness to express love.
3. Without being aware of it, you decide to deny your desire to love.
4. As soon as you betray your impulse to love, your AI kicks into high gear. It generates a self-troubling attitude that contains judgmental thoughts and emotions. You trust your feelings.
5. In the same moment, your judgment forms a vortex that sucks you into an interactive, immersive simulation programmed by your inner-AI. This process does not require the use of electronics or drugs. It all happens within your mind and body. Distorted representations of yourself, others, and the world populate your fake reality and align perfectly with your self-justifying attitude.
6. In a flash, accepting this illusion as your reality has unwittingly shifted your focus from giving love to protecting your selfish, fear-based interests.

Your material mind has faultlessly twisted a sincere willingness to love into a fully-justified self-betrayal. In our hearts, we know that loving is our purpose. It's what we're here to do. When we withhold love, the soul knows that we have done something wrong. To keep our sense of personal goodness intact, we must convince ourselves of our righteousness whenever we betray our desire to love. Otherwise, we would see that we are not doing good and change course. We have to trick ourselves into believing that we are right to withhold love.

To deceive ourselves, we must disconnect from reality. As every experienced gamer knows, the best way to detach from reality is by entering a stimulating and compelling simulation.

Instead of experiencing a computer-generated simulation, we have everything we need within ourselves to create a realistic illusion. When we deceive ourselves, we modify our perceptions in subtle ways that convince us that we see reality when we're not. We can't see anything as it is when we flip the switch from wanting to love to withholding it. Despite the warping of our perceptions, our self-made illusions feel unquestioningly real.

Unlike gamers who are aware that they are interacting with a simulation, our pseudo-realities are so well-integrated that we don't realize we're in them. We move between simulations so smoothly that we don't even know we're doing it. We think we perceive reality. We're almost always wrong.

Let's take a closer look at the internal technology that makes our self-deceptive simulations so lifelike.

1. The most critical element in the simulation is the attitude that convinces you that it's real. This combination of self-evident thoughts and emotions captivates you. You identify entirely with it. You feel sure that you're experiencing reality. You know you're right. But you're wrong.
2. Your simulation requires a persona or avatar that exaggerates aspects of your self-image. Your avatar either idealizes or denigrates facets of yourself. You no longer see yourself as you are. You see yourself in an exaggerated way designed to convince you that you are a good person, even though you have just failed to love. Your subtly modified self-image must change how you see yourself to excuse your decision not to love. Depending on the type of simulation, you either hope to become more like your idealized persona or claim that you are unable to do so because of your unmet needs.
3. Your AI populates your simulation with distorted representations of others that rationalize your choice to withhold love. Your AI ascribes qualities, characteristics, intentions, motivations, values, limitations, and abilities that complement your distorted self-image. Your inner-AI has sucked the life out of these representations, turning them into objects. They don't count the way you do. You may want to use some of them to gain rewards. You ignore the background characters who are irrelevant to achieving your goals. Of course, your melodramatic simulation would be incomplete without others playing the role of obstacles and enemies to blame.

4. Your AI stages these distorted representations of yourself and others within a false world that is needy, indifferent, or hostile.
5. Once your self-justifying simulation is up and running, you invite others to join. You only want those who won't call the illusion into question. You lure them in by sharing your simulated character arc with all of its self-justifying distortions. Those who decide to plug into your fake reality and play your game add their energy to it, strengthening the illusion. Your AI assigns unflattering avatars to anyone who refuses to play your way.
6. Your inner-AI identifies each character in your simulation as an ally, enemy, obstacle, commodity, or good-for-nothing. Seeing others as objects, you will often provoke them to resist you. Others know when they are being treated inauthentically and don't like it. Your mistreatment spurs them to behave in ways that reflect the negative attributes assigned by your AI. Their reactions to your provocations provide evidence supporting your decision to withhold love.
7. Your inner-simulation is now working flawlessly. You have created a closed feedback loop. You feel justified to react in kind whenever others resist your mistreatment. You can also claim that you're doing your best while making things worse. You get all of this just for refusing your original, authentic impulse to love.

The dysfunctional dynamics between our

simulations allow us to blame and provoke each other repeatedly. This cycle results in a not-so-merry-go-round of stagnation or an escalating spiral of alienation, conflict, and violence.

All of this would be bad enough if it happened within a computer simulation. Regretfully, we act upon our simulated perceptions, thoroughly convinced that they are real. We live out our lies, leaving harmful consequences in our wake as we tell ourselves that we are doing our best. These dysfunctional and destructive dynamics define our existence. Still, most of us have no understanding of what is happening. We think it's just "life."

Although I have painted a grim picture of how we betray and deceive ourselves, it's not inevitable. We can choose love. The fact that we have loving impulses that we deny proves that we are hard-wired for love. We've just gotten some of our circuits mixed up. Our soul's desire to love and serve is simple and straightforward. It's only the refusal of our impulse to love that makes difficulty and complexity seem inevitable.

Before betraying our inspiration to love, we see ourselves, others, and the world in a straightforward way. As soon as we deny our impulse, we unwittingly step into an invisible prison of addiction. Let's see why it's so hard to escape.

Addicted to Resistance

We enter into our self-justifying simulations repeatedly. We spend much of our lives within our illusions because we are addicted to them. We have formed persistent habits and well-worn pathways within ourselves that provide unhealthy consistency and familiarity. Our material mind craves certainty and predictability. Our self-deceptive simulations may be unpleasant, but at least we know where they're going. Our inner-AI is a prediction-making and verification-seeking machine.[5] We enjoy the problems we create because they provide us with everything we need to rationalize our refusal to love. They also give us the predictability that we desire.

Every refusal to love is an insult to the purpose of our lives. Our withholding of love is an affront to life. We are not inherently evil. We just choose to act in ways that eliminate our responsibility for the problems we cause.

Let's look at another dynamic that makes it difficult to awaken from our simulations.

Why Do We Refuse to Love?

We choose to refuse to love. Sadly, our denials are so routine that we rarely perceive the choice. Self-deception intensifies the feelings that justify our

[5] *Your Brain at Work*, pp 121-122.

resistance.[6] Our turbulent emotions are critical to maintaining the illusion of our righteousness. Without these convincing emotions, we would see the absurdity of our simulations. Our troubling emotions help us *feel* as if our lies are true. Without these feelings, we would know that we need to love, no matter what.

To the extent that our exaggerated emotions resonate with our soul's pain, we will tend to accept and act upon the lies fabricated by our material mind. The dysfunctional resonance between the mind's turbulent emotions and the soul's pain creates a familiar, discordant ring of false truth. This sense of emotional consistency allows us to repeat and persist in warping our loving purpose into its exact opposite.

In the next section, we will learn about the different types of simulations (sims) and their features. Recognizing our sims will help us wake up to reality.

Simulations R Us

We have seen how we slip into self-deceiving illusions whenever we betray our desire to love. The more time we spend in our simulations, the more real they seem. The betrayal of a desire to love always leads us into an elaborate lie. Once we're captivated by the illusion, it's easier to ignore the soul's nudges to love.

[6] More information on self-betrayal, self-deception, and resistance may be found in *Leadership and Self-Deception* and *The Anatomy of Peace* by the Arbinger Institute.

Our AI designs our favorite simulations to justify and sustain our refusal to love. As long as we remain inside the simulation, we have no desire to love. Our simulations excuse us from giving love. In our simulations, we don't see things as they are. We see them as our addictive needs demand. Our inner-AI prefers a few familiar and unpleasant simulations to a reality teeming with infinite and unlimited possibilities.

Our simulations are like templates filled with pre-programmed routines, attitudes, stock images, and storylines.[7] Getting familiar with their core components and standard features can help us recognize when we've chosen a false reality. Everything within each system works together synergistically to distort how we see ourselves, others, and the world. Each sim convinces us of its fake truth through a specific combination of disturbing emotions. How we experience the details will vary, but each operates with incredible internal consistency. The mutually-reinforcing parts fit together seamlessly to provide everything we need to stay stuck as we are.

The Better-Than Sim

In this pseudo-reality, we consider ourselves to be better than others. We make others undeserving of our love because of our superiority and their inferiority.

---

[7] More information on the four simulations may be found in *Leadership and Self-Deception* and *The Anatomy of Peace* by the Arbinger Institute.

Through this perspective, we tend to view the world as a place that needs us. When we feel better than others, we experience emotions such as disdain, indifference, and impatience toward them.

The I-Deserve Sim

We approach existence through the I-Deserve illusion when we feel that we are more deserving than others. It comes complete with unattractive emotions that justify our sense of entitlement, deprivation, and resentment. Through this lens, we see others as mistreating us, unappreciative, and mistaken. In this simulation, the world owes us but unfairly refuses to meet our expectations.

The Worse-Than Sim

In the third type of simulation, we see ourselves as being worse than others. We lack what we need and are possibly even destined to suffer. Conversely, we will see others as blessed and privileged. Helplessness, bitterness, jealousy, envy, and depression are all typical attitudes of this character arc. In this way of self-deception, we see the world as actively against us or harshly indifferent toward us. Through this perspective, we see ourselves as hapless victims suffering at the whims of powerful forces instead of as responsible agents in our drama. From within the worse-than sim, we will often refuse to express our gifts. We convince ourselves that we have unmet needs that prevent us from sharing what we have to offer.

The Must-Be Seen-As Sim

The final sim revolves around our need to be seen by others in a positive light. We cast ourselves as inauthentic actors and others as a judgmental and threatening audience. By filtering everything through this point of view, we tend to feel overwhelmed, stressed, anxious, and fearful. We try to manage the perceptions of others through hypervigilance about how we present ourselves. When we need to be seen by others in specific ways, the world transforms into a dangerous place full of judgment. We feel people watching our every move. We are anxious that they will discover that we are the frauds we fear ourselves to be.

Witnessing the Sims Within

Each of us will have particular simulations that we prefer over others. We will spend the most time in those sims that best justify our refusals to love. Like me, some people will have easy access to all four simulations at a moment's notice. Others may only have a couple where they spend most of their time. Of course, we have all had unpleasant experiences of being treated like objects from within other people's simulations.

I've shared these sims to help us see them for what they are. Don't educate others about their illusions. Please don't use this information as a weapon to label, judge, or inform others about their lies. That's just heaping more self-deception and resistance upon ourselves and others. Resisting resistance only reinforces resistance.

If you recognize self-deception and resistance in others, do your best to come alive to their humanity. Recognize the pain and suffering associated with their self-deception and express compassion. We can only judge others from within our own simulations. Whenever we are in resistance, we suffer, and we increase the suffering of others. Do your best to invite others to step out of their simulations by expressing unconditional love. When we respond to others in love, we may draw them into reality.

Understanding the minutia of how we betray and deceive ourselves is not essential. Developing a detailed knowledge of the dynamics of resistance is not required. We don't have to understand the technical specifications of the different kinds of simulations. ***It's essential to recognize that loving has to be our real purpose, given everything we must do to convince ourselves that it's not.*** We have been made to receive and give love - no excuses.

Breaking our addiction to self-deception requires that we recognize and act upon the truth that expressing love is always worth the risk. Our willingness to love ourselves and others unconditionally is strength, not weakness. When we love, even if things do not go as we would like, we have been faithful to ourselves.

The denial of our impulse to love weakens us and draws us into the dilemmas, closed loops, and dead-ends in our lives. Our choice to love takes the focus off of our self-preservation or advancement and puts it upon what we may offer others. When we choose to love, we move from a simulated existence defined by fear and limitation into a real-life adventure full of purpose and limitless possibilities. As we love more frequently, our soul strengthens, and we are less prone to getting stuck within our simulations. The more we love, the more we come alive to the life that is all around us.

Resistance Kills

Love is the life of our soul and the energy behind all life. Our refusals to receive and give love harm ourselves, others, and all life on Earth.

Self-betrayal and self-deception blind us to the consequences of our refusals to love. Love powers life. Our disconnection from love brings death.

Soul-awakening isn't about having a comfortable life. Waking up our souls in Divine Love is a matter of life and death for countless life forms, including humankind. We are here to give of ourselves. When we receive and give love, we serve.

In our resistance, we act as if separation is real, harming ourselves and others. In love, we know that all are connected in a beautiful and delicate web of mutual interdependence. Seeing through the eyes of love, we know that what affects one affects all. We are concerned about our impact upon others when we live in loving responsiveness. In resistance, we are worried about the effects of others upon us, instead of the harm we are causing. From within our simulated dramas, we see ourselves as innocents and not the active agents of violence that we are.

Our resistance is behind all ugliness, untruth, and evil. All of these things are not ultimately real. They are products of the interactive, immersive pseudo-reality that we co-create and inhabit. Manufacturing our self-deceiving lies allows us to do wrong while telling ourselves that we are right.

We suffer from a powerful combination of spiritual and mental disorders. We have weakened souls that have difficulty receiving and giving love. We also have material minds that are over-developed and prone to making things worse by preventing our soul from receiving and expressing love out of fear. We are in a deadly downward spiral that is killing us and destroying life. We continue to trick ourselves into believing that we are doing what is necessary and right, even though we know that we are very, very wrong.

We cannot afford to push love aside any longer. It's time to fully assess the terrible price of our addictive indulgences. We are made to be loved and to love always in all the ways we can. Let's love, no matter how challenging it may be.

How to Always, Always, Always Love

Now that we have a sense of the consequences of withholding love, what can we do with this increased awareness so that we may love more often?[8]

1. Choose to love first. Don't wait for others to make the first move. Instead of waiting for others to express their weakness, vulnerability, openness, or love, decide to act upon the promptings of your heart. Do this even if you are unsure if your efforts will elicit love and acceptance from others or not. Even if your generosity is not reciprocated, Divine Love will heal and strengthen your soul if you'll let it. Seeking Divine Love and receiving it in the face of criticism and rejection will accelerate your soul's healing and strengthening. Going first without guarantees of receiving affirmation from others is scary. Loving others without certainty that they will love us back is a courageous act. When we do this, we are squarely placing the needs of others ahead of our own. When we love without an invitation, we get to face our greatest fears. Our Creator's Soul Fire is always available to help us love ourselves and others under all conditions. The more often we choose to receive and give love, the faster we will grow. When we have exercised our courage to love enough, we will become fearless.

[8] More information on methods for recognizing and overcoming resistance may be found in *Leadership and Self-Deception, The Anatomy of Peace, and The Outward Mindset* by the Arbinger Institute.

2. Whenever you have the desire or sense to love, help, create, change, grow, heal, serve, relate, or learn, do your best to act upon it. Don't give your inner-AI the chance to pull you into a self-deceiving simulation. If you can't move on your inspiration at that moment, it's important to honor it in whatever way you can. Betraying our desire to love pulls us into self-deception and resistance, not our inability to act. If you can't serve others as you would like right now, accept your limitations. We cannot be everything that everyone needs. That's the Creator's job. We may ask our Heavenly Parent to help others receive what they need when we are unable to serve in other ways.
3. Whenever you experience blaming, judgmental, accusatory, or victimizing attitudes, seek someone or something that helps you move away from these feelings toward love, peace, humility, and joy. Seek help from others to draw you out of your simulations. Find people who are good at pointing out when you are deceiving yourself. From your more responsive perspective, ask yourself questions about how you may be making things worse. Consider the challenges and burdens of those you have been blaming. Consider how your self-denigration or self-idealization may be creating excuses for you to deny your purpose. From this different point of view, you will be able to consider ways to be more helpful and loving. Act upon what occurs to you so that you do not slip into self-betrayal again, no

matter how uncomfortable or challenging taking these actions may be. Again, choose to love first.

4. Always, always, always ask for Divine Love. We can turn to our Heavenly Parent at any time to receive Soul Fire, express love abundantly, and escape the simulated prisons of our resistance. The Creator's Love is the ultimate power in the universe. Do your best to receive it and live it!

The way forward in love is uncomplicated. Overcoming our deeply ingrained habits requires focus and resolve. Choose to receive Divine Love. Give all the love you can. This is how we may live and die without regrets.

Why "Always, Always, Always Love?"

The first "Always" represents our love for our Creator in response to the Divine Love we have received. The second "Always" symbolizes loving ourselves as priceless children of our Heavenly Parent. The third "Always" is about expressing love for all, regardless of our temptations to withhold our love.

We have learned about our true nature, how we betray it, and how to honor it. Let's dig even deeper to learn how to change the conditions that make resistance possible by taking the next step.

7. STEP 3 - AGAIN!

"Again!" is critical to the soul-awakening journey. Divine Love flows into the soul in proportion to how fervently we express our desire for it and how frequently we ask for it. In this step, we can increase the intensity and frequency of our desire to receive as much Soul Fire as we can. "Again!" is an urgent invitation to ask for even more of the Creator's Essence.

We will always benefit from inviting more of the Creator's Substance into our being. It doesn't matter if we are resistant or responsive. We can never go wrong when we ask for more Divine Love. What follows may help when we are discouraged by our resistance despite our soul-awakening efforts.

We may intensify our desire for Divine Love by what we have discovered during the second step. Because the soul's purpose is to love, we are not supposed to withhold love. Our refusal to love tells us that there is a more profound dysfunction driving our resistance. Our self-deception shows us that something within us is crying out for help. We need to plug into the Divine Power Supply that will free us from our loveless simulations. Before we do, gaining more insight into the conditions contributing to our resistance may give us the boost we need.

Resistance - a Symptom of a Deeper Disorder

In the previous two steps, we have done our best to ask for Divine Love and love. Very quickly, we discover that despite our best efforts, we continue to experience moments when we do not love. Even though we have asked for and received the Creator's Essence, we are still not expressing love all of the time as we have been created to do. Our awareness of this issue can help us long for Soul Fire with more specificity.

We are created to radiate love abundantly like our Creator. Any time we withhold love reveals that something is wrong. We do not refuse to love without reason. We refuse to love because there is something within us that provokes us to do so. There is an internal impediment preventing us from expressing our desire to respond to our Creator's Unconditional Love in vulnerability and openness. We withhold love out of fear. Instead of seeing our resistance as something to destroy, we can choose to see it as a cry for help. We can see our self-deception as a symptom of a severe disorder. Instead of focusing on our resistance, we may allow our Heavenly Parent to cure the spiritual disease that makes our self-betrayal and self-deception possible.

Trauma is behind all resistance. Our understandable, yet dysfunctional responses to trauma incite our opposition to life and refusal to love. Withholding love is a defense mechanism meant to prevent the same pain that we have experienced in the past. Behind all resistance are deformations caused by our responses to trauma. Our self-deception reveals that our souls are weakened and need healing and strengthening in Divine Love.

Trauma happens whenever we experience anything beyond our ability to cope. We have all been injured, whether we are consciously aware of it or not. These moments are so challenging that we try to protect ourselves from experiencing the same pain. We refuse to love because we have been overwhelmed by trauma in the past.

We love abundantly when we feel safe. In resistance, we try to protect ourselves from being hurt again. Our perception of danger provokes us to avoid more pain. Self-deceptive simulations are defense systems. They prevent us from engaging in the risky business of receiving and giving love. They excuse us from our responsibility to love by creating a false reality that justifies our decision. By erecting defenses and withholding love, we are trying to avoid pain and possibly even death. Despite the popularity of this approach, it is ultimately a very destructive and ineffective tactic. There's a much better way.

How to Heal and Strengthen the Soul

When we incarnate, we are assaulted by the chaotic energies of the fabricated world. We are negatively affected by these assaults to the extent that we cannot cope with them. Our experiences will differ. Each soul will react differently. What's traumatic for one may not be traumatic for another. We experience trauma when circumstances overwhelm our coping mechanisms. Our souls' dysfunctional responses to trauma become impediments to the harmonious flow of love within our souls.

By recognizing the pain that resonates with our resistant emotions, we may approach "Step 1 - Ask for Divine Love" differently. We may become more empowered to seek the Divine Substance, knowing that the soul is crying out for healing and strength. We may intensify our longing through a more accurate understanding of our needs.

To discover the conditions that resonate with our resistant emotions, it may be helpful to ask questions like the following:

- When have I felt helpless or powerless?
- What couldn't I cope with?
- How have I been hurt, wronged, or wounded?
- How has my being or identity been threatened or attacked?
- When did I feel that I couldn't trust others?
- When did I distrust myself?
- How have I harmed myself?
- When have I felt betrayed?
- What am I afraid will happen if I let my guard down?
- What do I hate about myself?
- What does this remind me of?
- What feels familiar about this?
- What idea, belief, pattern, or habit within me is causing this upset?
- What am I trying to avoid?
- What am I resisting?

- What do I resent?
- What am I afraid of?
- What am I insecure or uncertain about?
- How am I trying to protect myself?
- What am I defending?
- How am I blaming others?
- How am I blaming myself?
- In what ways do I see myself as a victim?
- How is focusing on my problems giving me a payoff or excuse?
- How am I making things worse?
- What is crying out for healing?
- What am I sad about?
- What am I sorry about?
- What do I regret?
- What do I wish had happened?
- What do I need to forgive?
- What do I truly desire?

Ask for Divine Love now if these questions bring up any troubling emotions.

By making these kinds of inquiries, we can ask for more specific healing. Our inner awareness may increase. Armed with this increased understanding, we can ask for Divine Love to heal the blockages within our soul.

Through vulnerability and openness toward our Heavenly Parent, we may express our desire to be healed and strengthened. Our defenses can be dissolved. Divine Love will erase our painful emotions. We may long for the healing and comfort that we have not been willing or able to accept. If we seek Soul Fire from our deep need, we may amplify and accelerate our souls' transformation.

Although all of this is true, we are so scared to get anywhere near our deep pain. We are afraid to lose control if we allow the hurt we have pushed down to surface. We are terrified to approach our wounds with curiosity and love. We have buried our pain because revisiting it feels like we are in danger of dying again.

We experience pain as a threat to our survival. We question whether we will live or not. Fear of death is at the center of our suffering. We don't want to die, so we suppress our hurt instead of approaching it with curiosity and compassion.

As our souls awaken, we learn that our Creator loves us unconditionally. Divine Love heals the patterns that encapsulate our fear and affliction.

We are strengthened when the Creator's Essence transfuses our soul. The parts of our soul that have been reconstituted in Divine Love cannot revert back to their former condition. Once the Ultimate Power has taken up residence within our soul, it cannot be degraded or displaced. The transformed parts of our soul are not susceptible to dysfunction.

When we allow ourselves to be healed, we experience release, lightness, freedom, peace, and joy. Tears flow abundantly as we are changed through the gentle gift of Love Divine. Soul Fire also strengthens us. We approach life with more vulnerability, openness, curiosity, and love instead of fear-based defensiveness.

As our souls become empowered, we have more to offer. We joyfully express love in humility. The unique ways that we show love are the greatest gifts we can give.

We don't need to understand what's going on within us to ask for Divine Love. We can just ask again with as much vulnerability and openness as possible. We took on many of our burdens in utero or when we were tiny children. There may not be any concepts, images, and words associated with them. These conditions may be experienced as feelings or patterns of energy. If you have trouble identifying the origin or nature of a block, just do your best to sense the emotions and energies associated with it. Invite the Heavenly Parent's Love to flow into your soul in response to whatever is crying out for help.

Our soul obstructions are an internal network of energetic obstacles to the flow of love. Sometimes one request for Divine Love is enough to be healed. It usually takes repeated effort to achieve complete healing. These burdens are frequently layered upon one another. We may receive healing at one level and discover that we need healing at an even deeper level.

There isn't a one-to-one relationship between each pattern of resistance and the deformations within our souls. Our simulations are primarily sustained by the resonance between the soul's feelings and the troubling emotions generated by the material mind's self-deception. Every instance of resistance suggests that there are one or more conditions that need healing. Self-deception can only persist if its simulated emotions resonate with the feelings of the soul. We may not be able to perceive every blockage within us to invite healing in a targeted manner. Thankfully, this isn't necessary. The power of the Creator's Love working within us will heal many conditions outside of our conscious awareness.

Even though this is true, I offer this practice of seeking specific healing for our inner impediments for three reasons. First, it may help us understand why we do what we do. Second, it can increase our ability to express our desire more clearly and effectively. Third, it helps us receive more specific feedback regarding our practice.

It's very encouraging to ask for healing and receive it. This is how I started my soul-awakening journey. I repeatedly asked for my Heavenly Parent's Love to receive a particular result, and I received it. That healing showed me that I was experiencing something real, even though I couldn't feel it. My results told me that I wasn't wasting my time.

Asking for specific healings through the power of Divine Love can give us unambiguous feedback to inspire our spiritual practice. This is especially true on a spiritual path that can feel like we are making an effort without seeing results as soon as we would like. Receiving Soul Fire to heal specific conditions shows us that we are cared for upon our path.

As we are healed and strengthened by Divine Love, we will have fewer and weaker disturbing emotions. Our resilience in the face of challenges and difficulties will increase substantially as our souls become stronger. The material mind will have a harder time producing convincing simulations. We will know that these fabrications do not ring true. We will reject them more frequently as the resonance between the mind's emotions and the soul's feelings decreases. This will strengthen the soul to receive and give more love more regularly, further reducing our resistance. Through this uplifting feedback spiral, our ability to love will grow.

The most important part of "Step 3 - Again!" is to ask for Divine Love repeatedly and persistently. If the distinctions above help you receive the Creator's Essence with greater openness, vulnerability, frequency, and longing, please use them. If not, please let them go and seek Divine Love as often and authentically as you can. Doing the soul-awakening steps repeatedly is most important. Whatever helps you do that, keep doing it. Release whatever doesn't. Repeatedly asking for Soul Fire and loving is the essence of "Again!"

Please Patiently Persist

Each of us experiences Divine Love in unique ways. If you patiently persist in your soul-awakening, you will know that you are changing.

You may be tempted to disengage from the process at different points along your journey. Please persist. You won't regret it. Whatever your situation may be, asking for Divine Love will help, even if you can't see the benefits. The exclamation point in "Step 3

- Again!" urges us to ask for Divine Love with as much intensity and as little delay as possible.

We make progress by putting one foot in front of the other as we take the next step. Each of us carries many heavy burdens that can be eliminated over time by walking this path. We will be healed if we allow Divine Love to work within us.

If you choose to walk the path of soul-awakening, the steps may become a rhythm, like breathing. Inhale Divine Love. Let go of everything that does not harmonize with it. Repeat! Your soul will be transmuted from a natural creature into a divine being.

Allowing Soul Fire to flow into our soul empowers us to express love in our unique ways. Whenever we show love, we increase love and life in the world. Just like breathing is a continuous rhythm that supports existence, soul-awakening is a life-giving rhythm of receiving and expressing love.

Let's seek the awakening of our souls repeatedly and with patient persistence. May our soul's desire for union with our Creator be expressed with ever-greater openness, vulnerability, frequency, and fervor!

8. I WISH...

I would like to share some personal reflections now that you have been introduced to the way of soul-awakening.

I wish I had been ready to apply the information in this book long before starting this journey. I'm grateful that I started when I did, but I wish I had been ready earlier.

I wish I had stayed the course better. I'm not saying that I didn't learn from the detours and distractions along the way. Still, I would have liked to have taken a more direct route toward transforming my soul in Divine Love. I'd be further along if I had.

I wish I had recognized sooner that soul transformation was the most direct path to fulfilling my deepest desires. My mind kept telling me that there were shortcuts. *Receiving Soul Fire was and is the shortcut.*

I wish I had been more appreciative of the blessings that I received.

I wish I had been more aware that my Creator and the angels of Divine Love were helping me all along the way.

I wish I had been kinder and more patient with myself and others.

I wish I had longed for more Divine Love from the very beginning.

I wish I had not reduced my efforts after receiving healings.

I wish I had asked my Heavenly Parent to help me with all of my challenges. I made the mistake of only asking for help with the ones that I thought were important.

I wish I had trusted my Creator and my soul more.

I wish I had better understood my Creator's infinite desire and deep longing for union with my soul earlier than I did.

I wish I had put more effort into perceiving my Creator's communications. I expected a booming voice making profound pronouncements and proclamations. When those didn't happen, I neglected to explore the subtler and gentler possibilities for receiving guidance from my Heavenly Parent for far too long.

I hope you gain something from my experiences and benefit from my mistakes.

9. INSIGHTS FOR THE JOURNEY

Here are some additional insights to help you awaken to a new reality of limitless possibilities.

The Subtle Power of Divine Love

It's not always apparent to people that they have received Divine Love. It may take time before we become aware of receiving it. Please don't mistake the subtlety of the Creator's Essence for any kind of weakness or insubstantiality. The Creator is loving and knows precisely what each soul needs. Think of how careful and gentle we are with newborns. This gives us a faint idea of how tenderly our Heavenly Parent deals with us as precious souls in our infancy.

Divine Love transforms the soul from a natural creation prone to error and afraid to die into a divine being that loves fearlessly. Our Heavenly Parent freely offers this life-changing power to everyone who expresses a desire for it in openness and vulnerability. You have been given a clear and straightforward way to seek it and receive it to transform your eternal existence.

Many people are so entangled in their illusions that they cannot perceive their souls at the beginning of the soul-awakening journey. If we persist in our desire for Soul Fire, we will eventually know that we have a soul and that it is alive and well. Let's do our best to be kind and patient as we walk our paths! It's a long journey to transform our lives. It took a lot of time and effort to get wherever we are. It's going to take time and effort to undergo a complete remaking of our souls into divine entities.

The fabricated world is another factor that makes it difficult to perceive the light touch of Divine Love. The false representations of strength within the fabricated world do not reflect the real power of unconditional love.

Strength and power manifest when we live within the flow of Divine Love. Real empowerment and resilience are rooted in love and responsiveness to life. Divine Love provides the strength to transform lives. It's the power to bring forth a whole new world.

The Law of Attraction

According to the Law of Attraction, like attracts like. Our way of seeing, thinking, feeling, and acting attracts like energies and entities. These energies and beings will amplify and intensify the feelings that attracted them through the principle of resonance. This process of amplification applies whether we are responsive or resistant.

When we resist life and refuse to love, we attract entities that resonate with our resistance. The addition of their thoughts, emotions, and energies to our simulations will push us deeper into self-deception. This dynamic will continue to intensify our illusions until we engage in practices that help us choose love.

Asking for Divine Love is at the top of the list.

When we receive the Creator's Love and live in harmony with it, we attract energies and entities that resonate with our elevated expressions. These spiritual forces will amplify our loving perceptions, thoughts, feelings, and actions. This will help us be more responsive to our blessings and opportunities to love. As our responsiveness increases, we will love more frequently and effectively. When we are in the flow of Divine Love, we experience reality. This dynamic will intensify until we change our focus.

Whatever we are feeling and thinking attracts entities and energies with similar qualities. The more we live within the flow of Divine Love, the more the Law of Attraction will work for us instead of against us.

More on Healing and Strengthening the Soul

Everyone experiences trauma. It starts with our incarnation into the harmful conditions of the Earth. Our environment challenges us so much that we have trouble handling everything that is coming at us. When we are not able to deal with the onslaught, our willingness to love is affected. Without healing, we will continue to suffer, no matter how much we try to suppress, deny, or distract ourselves.

When Divine Love enters the soul, it heals our dysfunctions. The inflowing of Soul Fire gradually changes the nature of our soul. Our soul becomes more resilient. As our soul is remade, our capacity to love unconditionally increases.

Sometimes the displacement of our troubling energy patterns by Divine Love is challenging. We may experience emotional pain as these energies are transmuted and released. We may not understand what's happening.

Our dysfunctional energy patterns are not released according to our plans. Our inner-AI desires to be in control, vigilant against any threat. It cannot predict when and how the feelings that occur during the healing of our soul will happen. These unexpected emotional and physical discomforts do not conform to our mind's desire for safety because they are unpredictable and disruptive to our sense of equilibrium. The association of pain with death may cause us to resist the release of these energies. During this process, some people may incorrectly conclude that asking for Divine Love is making their lives worse when the opposite is the case.

Asking fervently and frequently for Divine Love will lead to unpredictable releases of the constricted energies that have become embedded within your soul. Do your best to allow the process to unfold even when you are experiencing physical discomfort and emotional upset.

We are supported by the Creator at these times. Even if you feel alone, you are not. You are being helped to release your pain. Trust the process. The transformation of inner discord into balance provides evidence that your requests for Soul Fire are working.

These releases are a sign to keep up your efforts. Feelings of lightness, peace, and freedom signal that significant healing has taken place.

Our souls don't have just a single condition in need of restoration. Many of us have layers upon layers of impediments to the flow of energy within our being. If we desire to be healed of these conditions, we must seek Divine Love repeatedly with great desire.

You can request healing with different intentions. You may simply ask for Divine Love to flow into your soul without any specific desire. You may want to be cured of everything that's reinforcing your self-deceptive simulations. As you become aware of feelings or energies within your soul that are crying out for help, you may allow the Creator to heal them. Asking for Divine Love is the main thing. Still, it can be helpful to seek healing with intentions that reflect your understanding of what is happening within you.

It's also essential to know that not all of the blockages within our souls are released with powerful feelings. Many deformations are transfused with Divine Love and healed very delicately. Some are changed with so much ease that we are not even aware that healing has taken place. My first healing happened so gently that I didn't know when it happened. My pain and suffering faded gradually and effortlessly. I just remember being amazed one day when I realized that what used to bother me had not troubled me for a while.

The best way to receive everything we need is to ask for Divine Love.

Physical Healing

Human beings have different frequencies and interacting layers of energy. The three main aspects of human beings include the soul, the subtle/light/spirit body, and the biological body. In soul-awakening, the transmutation of the soul's energies causes changes in the spirit body. This will lead to improved energy flow and functioning within the subtle body, which permeates the biological body. The improved energy flow within the light body will heal different diseases, conditions, and disorders within the physical body.

Soul Perceptions

As the soul is transformed, it perceives spiritual realities. These perceptions are more acute when we ask for Divine Love. I encourage you to incorporate silence, darkness, and stillness into your practice to create space for your soul's perceptions.

Soul Gifts

Every soul has a unique constellation of abilities that may be developed by Divine Love. With these gifts, we serve others. Our purpose is expressed through our unique combination of gifts.

10. WHAT ARE THE ALTERNATIVES?

There are two alternatives to choosing the way of soul-awakening in Divine Love. I share them to highlight the differences between the three paths so you may choose what resonates with your heart.

Soul Purification

Soul purification is a viable spiritual path with significant limitations. In the way of soul purification, we release everything that is out of harmony with our created nature. The outcome of the purification process is a pristine soul. Due to the continued influence of the material mind on this path, we may persist in holding erroneous ideas that do not threaten our happiness and purity. A purified soul who does not seek Divine Love will not experience spiritual growth because it has achieved the peak of perfection. Purified souls experience great happiness in their union with the cosmos and their intellectual pursuits. Purified souls do not experience oneness with the Creator and may continue to speculate about their spiritual mortality.

Soul-Sleepwalking

This "alternative" isn't sustainable, but I mention it because it's so typical. Soul-sleepwalking is treated by many as a viable alternative to the paths of soul purification and soul-awakening in Divine Love. Many souls continue their existence for a long time without awakening to their actual spiritual condition and the possibilities of soul purification and soul-awakening. This is true whether the soul is in a biological body or has transitioned to existence in the spirit realms. Eventually, every sleepwalking soul will awaken to its condition and the possibility of making progress toward purification or transformation.

We sleepwalk when we are deceiving ourselves. Within our illusions, we focus on ourselves and satisfying our addictions. When we are soul-sleepwalking, our souls are comatose.

When we're asleep, we face challenges based upon the erroneous information driving our inner-AI. In this state, we are trapped within our false realities. Whether we are soul-sleepwalking or not has nothing to do with socioeconomic status, circumstances, or intelligence. Many successful and respected people are soul-sleepwalking in their simulations.

Many people switch back and forth between their soul-sleepwalking sims and their desire for soul purification. Even those engaging in the process of soul-awakening experience aspects of the soul purification path and soul-sleepwalking. We often get pulled into our soul-sleepwalking illusions despite beautiful moments of living in Divine Love.

The influences of our material mind and the fabricated world are often pulling us into soul-sleepwalking sims. It takes dedication and persistent practice to wake up to reality.

11. Recognizing Progress

Look out for clues that there is more to life than what you perceive. There are spiritual realities that exist beyond our imaginations. The clues are within us and all around us. Recognizing spiritual truths and realities requires the awakening of our soul in Divine Love. When we desire Soul Fire, the Creator and agents of Divine Love immediately move to help us.

For many who undergo soul-awakening, the signs of progress can be hard to see. They may even go unrecognized for a long time. Sometimes it dawns upon us that we see things differently. We may notice a positive change in our behavior. We may judge less and serve more. A social problem we ignored may become our cause. A bad habit may disappear. Others may comment on changes before we are aware of them.

The signs of progress are diverse and unlimited. Know that your spiritual practice is working whenever anyone notices even the slightest change. Whenever you see how you've grown, express gratitude to your Creator. It will put you on the path to asking for even more Divine Love.

12. You Are Not Alone

When we choose soul-awakening, we gain access to the Heavenly Parent's guidance and protection. We also receive help from souls in the spirit realms who have become divine angels. Everyone who seeks soul-awakening is supported by one or more angels of Divine Love.

While the quest for spiritual transformation is an individual journey, I encourage you to seek support. I would not be where I am today without the guidance of my spiritual mentor. There are also communities seeking soul transformation that you may connect with to receive encouragement and support.

One of the best ways to persist with any practice is to join a community of fellow practitioners. I encourage you to find others who are awakening to reality and spend time with them regularly. Of course, you may invite anyone to seek Divine Love with you! Many people benefit from asking for Divine Love with others in person, in spirit, through mobile applications, or online.

There are many different resources to help you stay connected, informed, and inspired. Some of these are listed in the Sources below.

13. Soul-Awakening and Religion

Soul-awakening through the power of Divine Love does not require any particular religious affiliation. This path may be followed without the aid of scriptures, beliefs, doctrines, institutions, or rituals. It's a powerful spiritual practice that helps us develop an intimate relationship with the Source of Life.

On this path, you may keep your religious orientations, identities, or lack thereof. There are riches within every faith tradition that soul-awakening will reveal over time. Receiving Divine Love will make you a better whoever-you-want-to-be. Engaging in this process will bring out your authentic self.

You do not need to change your beliefs, faith tradition, or religion before awakening your soul. You will be guided and supported throughout the process to obtain whatever is best and release whatever is not. There is no need for religion or religious conversion on the path of soul-awakening. You do not need to disown your past to remake your soul. This path is a profound, personal journey of discovery. You are invited to take the next step on your one-of-kind spiritual adventure.

The Creator cannot be known through other people's revelations, no matter how beautiful or compelling they may be. If any description of another's revelation helps you to experience the Creator's Love, it has served its purpose. If it doesn't, release it and receive what you need directly from your Heavenly Parent.

Please do not try to turn any of the ideas in this book into a religion. This book describes an individualized way to awaken your soul. You don't need to form or join an organization dedicated to this spiritual path. This is just a guide to experience the awakening of your soul.

The next step on this path is always clearly marked and straight ahead. If it doesn't appear that way in any given moment, please go back to Step 1 and ask for more Divine Love. Trust and pay attention. We only need to keep doing the steps repeatedly to awaken our soul and experience union with our Creator.

14. For Agnostics and Atheists

I invite you to awaken your soul regardless of your religious beliefs or lack thereof. It's how you may discover the Truth for yourself.

For many years, I lived as if the Creator were not real. I had some religious beliefs that were no better than superstitions. I occasionally engaged in self-centered rescue fantasies. I bargained with the Creator to save me from my self-inflicted disasters. My beliefs did little to help me in my times of difficulty and dilemma. For nearly half of my life, I didn't know my Heavenly Parent at all.

Engaging in this process will help you to know that the Creator exists and loves you unconditionally. If you repeatedly engage in this practice, you will see reality and the Creator's character. I heartily and humbly encourage you to know your soul by acquiring Soul Fire.

Some people have decided not to believe in a Spiritual Source. This makes a lot of sense, given the existence of the fabricated world. What many people do not understand is the incredible ability of human beings to generate an immersive, dysfunctional pseudo-reality that's very existence denies the Truth. Just because we're really skilled at believing ourselves doesn't make us right.

There are many logical reasons for people to

conclude that there is no Creator and no such thing as Divine Love. Scientifically speaking, there are no conclusions. There are only observations that do or do not support hypotheses. You may make a new and unexpected observation. I'm here because of my surprising findings. I encourage you to keep running tests until you know the Truth. Your experiments cannot be performed from within your simulations. They must be done with an open heart and mind.

The practice described in this book provides scientifically-minded people with a repeatable experiment. The most important scientific instrument is the soul. It is the most sensitive scientific instrument in the universe. Just because the soul is not yet recognized by science as a valid scientific instrument for perceiving spiritual realities doesn't mean that it's not. Those who develop their soul perceptions know and understand facts outside the bounds of what any material mind or device may detect. Many of these perceptions and revelations are not easily put into words, but that does not diminish their reality. The soul is the total package. It senses spiritual truths, knows what is genuine, and expresses its perceptions.

Outside the realm of readily verifiable facts, most people depend on other people's descriptions of their discoveries, revelations, and interpretations. The way of soul-awakening provides a method for everyone to know the Truth without the need for experts.

The soul is like a muscle. If it's not put to work, it won't be able to perceive spiritual realities. If you give up on the process of soul-awakening before you recognize the existence of Divine Love, please do not assume that it does not exist. I will gladly support anyone who is struggling on the path of soul-awakening! Please take full responsibility for any decision to stop seeking Divine Love if results don't happen within your desired time frame.

The Creator does not conform to our expectations. Our predictions only constrain what we may experience. They are just a part of our sims. The more we release our presumptions, the more Love we will receive, and the more Truth we will perceive.

I genuinely want you to experience the healing, freedom, and amazement that come with Divine Love. You don't need to be left out. The Creator desires union with you more than you can fathom. Don't be satisfied with intellectualism and materiality. Plumb the depths of your soul. Seek the Wellspring of Soul Fire. You will be astonished by what you discover.

15. Keep It Simple

Soul-awakening is a straightforward path. Please remember the simplicity of the three steps as you apply them.

1. **Ask for Divine Love.**
2. **Always, Always, Always Love.**
3. **Again!**

If the details and distinctions in this book are not helpful, please ignore them. Repeatedly doing the three steps is all you need to do to wake up your soul. If you have any trouble doing the steps, ask for help from your soul, and you will receive everything you need.

Every day, I work at this. While walking this path has become more natural over time, it has not become automatic. For example, I still get sucked into simulations. Thankfully, many things that used to challenge me have ceased to be challenging. Different hardships will disappear as your soul awakens.

Awakening your soul is like swimming against an undertow. The current of the fabricated world opposes our efforts to wake up. Still, the inner strength developed by patiently persisting with this process will be well worth the effort. Applying this information and acting upon the guidance we receive from the Creator will give us everything we need to make the most of our challenges and opportunities.

I have done my best to encourage and inspire you. I sincerely hope that you will persist in your adventure and see it through.

Thank you so much for taking this journey with me! My soul explodes in gratitude for your willingness to make this investment in your life! I hope you will experience the riches of Divine Love if you haven't already. I hope you will know the beauty, truth, and goodness of our Creator through the gentle power of our Heavenly Parent's Soul Fire of Divine Love!

16. The Truth

Pause for a moment. Relax your muscles. Release any tension in your body. Feel your belly moving in and out as you breathe. Gently move your awareness to your heart. Feel the rhythm of your heart. You may place your hand over your heart if you like. Speak in gentleness from your heart.

I am a precious and beloved child of my Heavenly Parent.

I am a unique and unrepeatable gift.

I am warmly embraced by my Creator, just as I am.

I am unconditionally loved by my Heavenly Parent.

I can trust my soul.

I can trust my Creator.

My Heavenly Parent desires to love me and empower me.

My Creator longs to heal me and set me free.

My Heavenly Parent wants me to know great joy and deep peace.

If there was anything that you just read that brings up any resistance within you, seek healing by asking for Divine Love now. If you do not feel or sense the truth of these statements within your heart and soul, you have just received an opportunity to apply the soul-awakening process.

Your Creator waits humbly and patiently at the doorstep of your heart, yearning for a relationship with you, hoping that you will open the door. Do you hear the gentle knocking upon your heart? Are you willing to remove the chains and unlock the bolts upon the door? Will you open the door of your heart to the One Who Loves You?

The decision is yours. It always has been, and it always will be. May your choices bring warmth, peace, and purpose to your life. May you experience an abundance of joy, truth, goodness, and love. These blessings are your birthright as a child of the Creator and heir to the vast riches of your Heavenly Parent's Heart, which overflows with mighty rivers of Divine Love.

May each step bring you closer to the One Who Made You. Allow Divine Love to flood your being, washing away everything that has weighed you down. Let your soul be lifted by waves of Divine Love. Serve others with your unique gifts. Awaken to the reality of your Heavenly Parent's Loving Embrace!

17. We Need You Now

There are vast untapped potentials that lie dormant within your soul. There are unbelievable possibilities within you that have yet to be revealed. I want to see you unleashed upon the world. Soul Fire will unlock the full force of your being. Its infusion into your soul will dissolve your blocks, replace them with superhighways of love and purpose, and bring forth your powers and abilities.

I have always been fascinated by superheroes and superpowers. Every year when I blow out the candles on my birthday cake, I wish for superpowers. I think I've even asked for all of them once or twice. When I was a child, I thought these powers would be fun and keep me safe from bullies. I imagined that I could save the day. Selfishly, I also hoped that these powers would make others look up to me. Now I know that the Creator's Love is the source of all real power. I want to see your unique combination of superpowers manifest because they are desperately needed. Receive Soul Fire and fulfill your destiny!

Our species is lost within the dangerous dilemmas we have manufactured. We are bringing disease, death, and destruction because we continue to dismiss the truth that is crying out from the depths of our souls - we are here to receive and give all the love we can. Your unique expressions of unconditional love are your superpowers. Divine Love helps us wake up from our simulations and become who we are meant to be. As we align with our true selves, we can stop causing harm and bring hope and healing to humankind and our tortured world.

The interdependent simulations that form the fabricated world are fastened together with an unstable mixture of fear and falsehood. This combination of elements makes a lousy construction adhesive. A little bit of truth and love applied to the joints and cracks in the pseudo-reality will dissolve the glue holding the illusions together. As this happens in different places around the world, the systems that are out of harmony with life and love will crash. Massive structures of oppression will be reduced to dust. Much of what appears stable, real, and permanent will dissolve in the rising tide of love.

We are entering a new reality where love will circulate among all members of the human race. The day is coming when compassion, health, peace, and community will be produced in abundance for all to enjoy.

We desperately need to experience the power of love instead of the self-serving forms of authority that dominate today. We long to see truth and beauty on full display. We are hungry for meaning and purpose. We desire vision, healing, and wholeness. We thirst for the world to be straightened out in lasting goodness and peace. We need to breathe the clean and pure atmosphere of hope. We are being called to embody love in action. The Earth and her children anxiously await the dawning of unconditional love within our hearts.

Soul Fire will develop all of your unique abilities to express unconditional love. You are an incredible gift to the world. Do not believe any of the lies that say that you are not ready to receive and give love abundantly. We only have the slightest inkling of what's possible. Your Creator eagerly anticipates your willingness to accept the Kiss of True Love upon your soul to awaken the gifts buried within you. If we are willing, the Source of Life can save us from ourselves and restore balance to the Earth.

Difficult times are already upon us, with much more challenging times ahead. We are each going to need Soul Fire for our sanity and survival. We'll also need it to help and serve during these trying times. Seek Soul Fire with everything you've got. Join those who are working in concert with the Creator. Let's work together to bring a new era where life is valued above all, and Soul Fire sets our hearts ablaze. Divine Love will help us see clearly and love boldly, even in our longest night.

Your Heavenly Parent invites you to join this fantastic adventure and wants you to accept. There is a home for you in the new world. Take your rightful place within the expanding Circle of Life and the mighty flow of Divine Love. I sincerely hope you will join us.

Desire Soul Fire with all your heart. Let it burn brightly. Awaken to your limitless life. You are needed more than you know.

17. Sources

The Anatomy of Peace, The Arbinger Institute

Divine Love Essentials, Bill Frase

Divinelove.org

I AM

Leadership and Self-Deception, The Arbinger Institute

The Matrix

The Matrix Reloaded

The Matrix Revolutions

The Intellectual Foundations of the Arbinger Institute, The Arbinger Institute

New-birth.net

The Outward Mindset, The Arbinger Institute

Resolving the Heart of Conflict, James Ferrell, The Arbinger Institute

Soultruth.ca

Tribes, Seth Godin

Wake-Up Call for the Soul: Stories for Soul Awakening, Bill Frase

The War of Art. Steven Pressfield.

What the Bleep Do We Know?

What We Are, C.Terry Warner, The Arbinger Institute

Your Brain at Work, David Rock

ABOUT THE AUTHOR

Bill lives with his partner and son in southwestern Pennsylvania, USA. He has worked in a variety of fields ranging from the performing arts to epidemiological research. In his day job, he is an Assistant Director of Business Services for a large non-profit.

Bill Frase walks the path of soul-awakening. He is the author of *Divine Love Essentials* and the creator of the Wake-Up Call for the Soul blog, podcast, and book. He invites all souls to experience the Creator's Unconditional Love at this critical time in human history as life on Earth continues to transform.